Arkansas

BY ANN HEINRICHS

Content Adviser: Michael Dougan, Ph.D., Arkansas State University, Jonesboro, Arkansas

Reading Adviser: Dr. Linda D. Labbo, Department of Reading Education, College of Education, The University of Georgia

COMPASS POINT BOOKS ✦ MINNEAPOLIS, MINNESOTA

Compass Point Books
3109 West 50th Street, #115
Minneapolis, MN 55410

Visit Compass Point Books on the Internet at www.compasspointbooks.com
or e-mail your request to custserv@compasspointbooks.com

On the cover: People paddle canoes up the Buffalo National River at the Steel Creek Access Area.

Photographs ©: Corbis/William A. Blake, cover, 1; Henry W. Robinson/Visuals Unlimited, 3, 5, 7;
Unicorn Stock Photos/Wayne Floyd, 8; John Elk III, 10, 20, 30, 42, 43 (top); Bill Draker/KAC
Productions, 11; Photo Network/Dennis MacDonald, 12; Arkansas Archeological Survey/
Peter Bostrom, 13; Courtesy of Mobile Area Convention and Visitors Bureau, 14; Corbis/Bettmann,
15, 18; North Wind Picture Archives, 16, 17; Hulton/Archives by Getty Images, 19, 32, 41; Corbis/
Tim Thompson, 22; Unicorn Stock Photos/Joe Sohm, 23, 46; Corbis/Buddy Mays, 24; U.S.
Department of Agriculture, 25; Unicorn Stock Photos/Eric R. Berndt, 26; Corbis/Carl Purcell, 28;
Frederick M. Brown/Getty Images, 29; Andy Lyons/Getty Images, 31; Corbis/Kevin Fleming, 33;
Unicorn Stock Photos/Travis Evans, 34, 47; Unicorn Stock Photos/Jim Argo, 35, 45; Corbis/Danny
Lehman, 37; Richard Thom/Visuals Unlimited, 38; Unicorn Stock Photos/B.W. Hoffmann, 40; Robesus,
Inc., 43 (state flag); One Mile Up, Inc., 43 (state seal); Gary M. Carter/Visuals Unlimited, 44 (top);
William J. Weber/Visuals Unlimited, 44 (middle); Comstock, 44 (bottom).

Editors: E. Russell Primm, Emily J. Dolbear, and Patricia Stockland
Photo Researcher: Marcie C. Spence
Photo Selector: Linda S. Koutris
Designer: The Design Lab
Cartographer: XNR Productions, Inc.

Library of Congress Cataloging-in-Publication Data
Heinrichs, Ann.
    Arkansas / by Ann Heinrichs.
        p. cm.— (This land is your land)
    Includes bibliographical references and index.
    Contents: Welcome to Arkansas!—Mountains, valleys, and plains—A trip through time—
Government by the people—Arkansans at work—Getting to know Arkansans—Let's explore
Arkansas!
    ISBN 0-7565-0339-6
    1. Arkansas—Juvenile literature. [1. Arkansas.] I. Title.
F411.3.H454 2004
976.7—dc21   2002012863

Table of Contents

4   **Welcome to Arkansas!**

6   **Mountains, Valleys, and Plains**

13   **A Trip Through Time**

20   **Government by the People**

24   **Arkansans at Work**

28   **Getting to Know Arkansans**

33   **Let's Explore Arkansas!**

41   Important Dates

42   Glossary

42   Did You Know?

43   At a Glance

44   State Symbols

44   Making Chicken-Fried Steak

45   State Song

46   Famous Arkansans

47   Want to Know More?

48   Index

NOTE: In this book, words that are defined in the glossary are in **bold** the first time they appear in the text.

Thomas Nuttall was a scientist from England. He explored Arkansas Territory in 1819. One day, he climbed Petit Jean Mountain.

"From the summit a vast **wilderness** presented itself," he said. He saw "lofty blue peaks" and "wild and romantic cliffs." There were "enormous masses of rock so nicely balanced as almost to appear works of art." The forests were full of wild turkeys and blooming flowers. Cotton, rice, corn, and wheat grew across the fertile plains.

Nuttall would see the same views if he visited Arkansas today. Arkansas's official nickname is the Natural State. It's known for its rugged mountains, lush forests, and wildlife. It has clear lakes and sparkling streams.

Arkansas has busy factories, too. They make foods, chemicals, electrical goods, and many other products. Arkansas produces more rice and chickens than any other state. Millions of tourists love to visit the Natural State. Now let's explore Arkansas. You're sure to love it, too!

▲ Sylamore Creek is one example of Arkansas's natural beauty.

Mountains, Valleys, and Plains

Arkansas lies in the south-central United States. The Mississippi River forms most of its eastern border. Across the river to the east are Tennessee and Mississippi. To the north is Missouri. Across the southern border is Louisiana. Oklahoma and Texas lie to the west.

Arkansas is a land of rugged mountains and fertile plains. Each of these landscapes covers about half the state. Imagine a line running through Arkansas from northeast to southwest. North and west of that line are mountains and hills. To the south and east are low plains.

The Ozark Mountains cover northwest Arkansas. Within these forested hills are valleys, lakes, and streams. The Ouachita *(WASH-a-taw)* Mountains reach into western Arkansas from Oklahoma. They're covered with pine and hardwood forests. Hot Springs is the major city in the Ouachita region. It grew up around the area's hot mineral springs. People once thought they could cure illnesses by bathing in or drinking the water from these springs.

▲ Tea Table Rocks at Home Valley Bluff are located in the Ozark Mountains.

The Arkansas River Valley cuts between these two mountain ranges. Little Rock and Fort Smith are the major cities along the river. Little Rock, the state capital, is in the center of the state. Fort Smith is on the Oklahoma border.

Fertile plains cover eastern Arkansas. This region is sometimes called the Mississippi **Delta,** or just the Delta. Much of the Delta was once swampy and tree-covered. This made the soil rich in minerals. Today, it is Arkansas's best farming area. Southwest Arkansas has thick pine forests. Beneath the surface are deposits of oil and natural gas.

▲ **An irrigated rice field near West Memphis in the Mississippi Delta region**

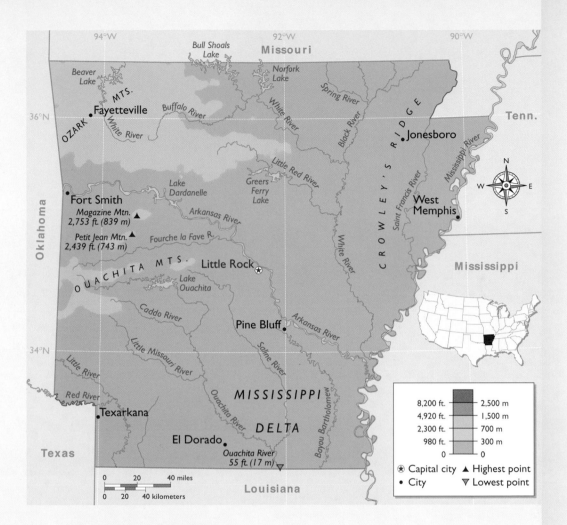

Bull Shoals
Lake

Missouri

94°W   92°W   90°W

Beaver
Lake   Norfolk
Lake

OZARK MTS.
Buffalo River   Spring River

Fayetteville
36°N   White River

White River   Black River   CROWLEY'S RIDGE

Jonesboro

Tenn.

Little Red River

Lake
Dardanelle   Greers
Ferry
Lake

Fort Smith
Magazine Mtn.
2,753 ft. (839 m)   Arkansas River   West
Memphis

Petit Jean Mtn.
2,439 ft. (743 m)   Fourche la Fave R.

OUACHITA MTS.   Little Rock

Lake
Ouachita

Mississippi

Caddo River

Pine Bluff   Arkansas River

34°N   Little Missouri River   Saline River

Little River

Red River   MISSISSIPPI

Texarkana   DELTA   Bayou Bartholomew

El Dorado

Ouachita River
55 ft. (17 m)

Texas

Ouachita River

Louisiana

N
W   E
S

8,200 ft.	2,500 m
4,920 ft.	1,500 m
2,300 ft.	700 m
980 ft.	300 m
0	0

⊛ Capital city   ▲ Highest point
• City   ▽ Lowest point

0   20   40 miles
0   20   40 kilometers

▲ A topographic map of Arkansas

One unique feature in the Delta is Crowley's Ridge. It
runs for 250 miles from the boot heel of Missouri southward
to Helena, Arkansas. The ridge rises above the land on either
side of it. Thousands of years ago, the Mississippi River ran
on the west side of the ridge. Today, it runs on the east side.

▲ **The Arkansas River runs through Fort Smith.**

Some plants on the ridge are not found anywhere else west of the Mississippi River.

The Arkansas, White, and Saint Francis Rivers empty into the Mississippi River. All these rivers deposit soil along their paths. That's why the Delta is so good for growing crops. The Arkansas River runs across the whole state. Many early explorers entered the region on this river. The Red River cuts across Arkansas's southwest corner.

Arkansas's lands are full of animals. Bears, deer, foxes, elk, and bobcats roam through the forests. Quail and wild turkeys scratch for insects on the ground. The lakes and sparkling streams abound with trout, bass, and other fish. Wetlands near the Mississippi River attract millions of waterbirds.

Summers in Arkansas are hot, and winters are cool. Winter can be harsh in the mountains. They get more snow and colder tem-

▲ **The great blue heron is one of many waterbirds living in Arkansas's wetlands.**

▲ Swimming in the Buffalo National River is a good way to cool off during the hot Delta summers.

peratures than other regions. Even in the summer, nights
in the mountains are cool. Summers are hottest in the
Delta region and the southwest.

A Trip Through Time

Many Native Americans once lived in Arkansas. The Dalton culture's Sloan Site is one of the oldest Native American cemeteries in North America. It dates back nearly ten thousand years. The **mounds** at Plum Bayou, now a state park, were an important ceremonial center.

The earliest inhabitants lived in small groups and moved constantly. They had only a few primitive stone tools. Over

▲ **People of the Dalton culture used stone spear points like this one.**

time, these people developed the bow and arrow, cultivated vast fields of corn, and built large cities.

When white explorers arrived, the Osage, who had lived in Missouri, began hunting in Arkansas. They hunted deer and bears in the forested hills. On the open plains, they hunted buffalo. The Caddo people farmed along the Red River. The Quapaw, who farmed in eastern Arkansas, fought with the Osage over hunting lands.

In 1541, Spanish explorer Hernando de Soto led an **expedition** into the area. He was looking for cities of gold. Unfortunately, his group brought diseases that killed most of the area's Native American population.

France claimed present-day Arkansas in 1682. It became part of France's vast Louisiana colony. Frenchman Henri de Tonti founded Arkansas Post in 1686. It was

▲ **Henri de Tonti founded Arkansas Post.**

Arkansas's first permanent European settlement. This land passed to Spain and back to France again. Finally, the United States bought the Louisiana Territory in 1803.

Shortly after this, the U.S. Army began moving Native Americans from eastern states. Cherokee and other groups were moved into Arkansas's Osage territory. Fort Smith was established in 1817. Soldiers there tried to keep peace among the different Native Americans groups.

Meanwhile, thousands of new settlers were pouring in. Some farmed the rich soil or cut forest trees for lumber. Others mined coal, lead, and iron. Huge cotton **plantations**

▲ Mining in Bauxite and other parts of Arkansas during the early 1900s brought many settlers to the state.

▲ Many people headed west from Arkansas in covered wagons to find gold in California.

that used slave labor arose along the Mississippi River. In the mountains, however, people had small farms. They hunted and fished for much of their food.

Arkansas became the twenty-fifth U.S. state in 1836. It was the third state west of the Mississippi River. In 1849, Americans began rushing to California to find gold. Many of them started out from Fort Smith and Van Buren, a neighboring town. There they loaded up their covered wagons with supplies for the long journey.

During this time, the country began arguing over slavery. Northern states wanted to abolish, or get rid of, slavery. Southern states wanted slaves to work the plantations. Along with other Southern states, Arkansas seceded, or separated, from the Union. They formed the Confederate States of America. Soon, the Civil War (1861–1865) broke out. In Arkansas, fierce battles took place at Pea Ridge and Prairie Grove in 1862. In the end, the Union won. Arkansas rejoined the Union in 1868.

▲ The Battle of Pea Ridge took place on March 8, 1862.

▲ Men working to join two oil pipelines at a highway near Little Rock

After the Civil War, the mineral bauxite was discovered near Little Rock in 1887. Oil was discovered near El Dorado in 1921. Businessman H. L. Hunt made a fortune selling the oil. Arkansans had a rough time in the 1930s, though. The Great Depression was sweeping the nation. Many people lost their jobs, farms, and homes. Arkansas also suffered a severe drought, or lack of rain.

Things began to improve during World War II (1939–1945). Thousands of troops trained in Arkansas. In the 1950s, U.S. public schools were ordered to integrate. This meant they were required to admit students of all races. Some Southern

▲ A National Guardsman helping a student with his bicycle during Arkansas's integration of its schools

states, including Arkansas, resisted the change. In 1957, federal troops went to Little Rock's Central High School. They made sure black students could safely enter the school.

In the 1960s, a massive project expanded the Arkansas River. Beginning in 1970, seagoing ships could travel up and down the Arkansas River. This change helped businesses move their products, or cargo.

Today, Arkansas's products range from chickens to computer software. Millions of tourists visit the state, too. Many people from other states are retiring in Arkansas. They all love Arkansas for its natural beauty.

Government by the People

Arkansas's state government works much like the U.S. government. It's divided into three branches—legislative, executive, and judicial. The three branches make a good balance. They make sure no branch gets too powerful.

The legislative branch makes the state laws. It also decides how the state will spend its money. Arkansas's lawmakers serve in the state legislature. The legislature has two houses, or parts. One is the 35-member senate. The

▲ **The state capitol in Little Rock**

▲ A geopolitical map of Arkansas

other is the 100-member house of representatives. They all meet in the state capitol in Little Rock.

The executive branch carries out the state's laws. Arkansas's governor is the head of the executive branch. Voters choose a governor every four years.

▲ Inside the courthouse at Pine Bluff, judges hear cases and make decisions.

The judicial branch is made up of judges and their courts. The judges decide whether laws have been broken. Arkansas's highest court is the state supreme court. Voters elect its seven judges.

Arkansas is divided into seventy-five counties. Each one elects a county judge as its chief executive. Most cities and towns have a mayor and a city council.

Arkansans are proud of their home-grown leaders. Arkansas governor William Jefferson Clinton became the nation's forty-second president. He served from 1993 to 2001. J. William Fulbright represented Arkansas in the U.S. Senate from 1945 to 1974. He was chairman of the Senate Foreign Relations Committee. Wilbur Mills served in the U.S. House of Representatives from 1939 to 1977. He was chairman of the House Ways and Means Committee.

▲ William Jefferson ("Bill") Clinton was the forty-second president of the United States.

How would you like to go digging for diamonds? Just head on over to Murfreesboro, Arkansas. It has a crater where visitors can mine for diamonds. They can keep whatever they find! Arkansas's leading mine product is invisible,

▲ Visitors who mine for diamonds at Crater of Diamonds State Park can take home whatever they find!

▲ Soybeans, like these growing near Blytheville, are an important Arkansas crop.

though. It's natural gas. Other important natural resources include bauxite, bromine, quartz, coal, oil, and barite.

Rice, soybeans, cotton, wheat, and corn are Arkansas's leading crops. Arkansas is the nation's top rice-growing state. Rice fields stretch across the moist land of the Delta region. Arkansas produces more chickens than any other state, too. Farmers also raise beef cattle, milk cows, turkeys, and hogs. Arkansas is a big fish-farming state. Catfish and trout are the major farm-raised fish.

Many of these farm products end up in factories. Food processing is Arkansas's top manufacturing activity. Some food plants process chickens or package rice. Others make

▲ The administrative offices of the Tyson chicken company are in Rogers.

animal food, bread, or canned fruits and vegetables. Trees from Arkansas's forests have many uses, too. Some are made into cardboard, paper, and pulp. Others are made into lumber, plywood, and other wood products. Arkansas factories also produce chemicals, electrical goods, machinery, rubber, and metals.

Most Arkansas workers hold service jobs. Instead of selling goods, they sell their services. Some work in stores such as Wal-Mart. Arkansan Sam Walton started the Wal-Mart chain of stores. Other service workers are in the wholesale trades. Wholesalers buy goods from farms or factories and resell them to stores where customers shop. Teaching, health care, and banking are some other service industries. These jobs all help Arkansas's residents, businesses, and visitors.

In 2000, there were 2,673,400 people in Arkansas. Little Rock, the state capital, is the largest city. Next in size are Fort Smith, North Little Rock, and Fayetteville.

Four out of five Arkansans are white. Many early pioneers came from Kentucky and Tennessee. Later, immigrants came from Germany, Italy, Poland, and other countries. Many of their descendants still live in Arkansas.

Almost one out of six Arkansans is African-American. In some eastern counties, more than half the residents are black.

▲ **Vacationers enjoying the Buffalo National River in a canoe**

Hispanics, Asians, and Native Americans live in Arkansas, too. Many Vietnamese people arrived in the 1970s.

Arkansas has produced many writers and musicians. Author Dee Brown wrote *Bury My Heart at Wounded Knee.* It tells the sad tale of Native Americans in the West. Maya Angelou is a poet and novelist. She's best known for *I Know Why the Caged Bird Sings.* Charles Portis wrote *True Grit,* a story

▲ **Writer Maya Angelou is from Arkansas.**

about a young girl's adventure in the West. Bette Greene's *The Summer of My German Soldier* is a popular book about World War II. Country music singers Johnny Cash and Glen Campbell came from Arkansas. Opera singer Barbara Hendricks did, too. Many African-American blues singers were from Arkansas. Scott Joplin, Florence Price, and William Grant Still, all African-Americans, were important American composers.

▲ Woodworking at the Ozark Folk Center

Blues music has a long history in the Delta region. Helena celebrates this tradition with the King Biscuit Blues Festival. Mountain View is a center for traditional Ozark folk arts. It holds the Arkansas Folk Festival in April. People display their quilts, wood carvings, hooked rugs, and baskets. The town holds a Fiddler's Championship in September.

Millions of ducks migrate through Stuttgart in the fall, so the town holds a World Championship Duck-Calling Contest. Speaking of champions, Hope has grown some champion watermelons. It holds a Watermelon Festival in August. If you have a champion toad, head for Conway. Its Toad Suck Daze festival includes a toad race.

The Tontitown Grape Festival celebrates the region's grape harvest. Fort Smith holds the Arkansas-Oklahoma Rodeo and a river festival in June. Yellville holds the National Wild Turkey Calling Contest. It's part of the Turkey Trot Festival.

"Wooo, Pig Sooie! Go Hogs Go!" That's the hog call for the University of Arkansas Razorbacks. They're named for wild pigs that once roamed the hills. The Razorbacks'

▲ The Arkansas Razorbacks football team is exciting to watch.

▲ Famous baseball player Jay Hanna "Dizzy" Dean played for the Saint Louis Cardinals.

basketball team won the national championship in 1994. The Razorbacks' football team often plays in holiday bowl games.

Plenty of sports stars have come from Arkansas. Baseball player Lou Brock was a champion base stealer. "Dizzy" Dean was a star pitcher. Both played for the Saint Louis Cardinals. Paul "Bear" Bryant was the "winningest" college football coach. He coached the University of Alabama's team, which is called the Crimson Tide. Scottie Pippen and Sidney Moncrief are Arkansas-born basketball stars. Pippen made his name with the Chicago Bulls. Moncrief played with the Milwaukee Bucks.

Let's Explore Arkansas!

Where would you find cave popcorn and **moonmilk?** They're all bizarre rock formations in Hurricane River Cave. It's one of the Ozarks's many underground **caverns.** They were hideouts for saber-toothed tigers, Native Americans, and Confederate soldiers. Bull Shoals Caverns is 350 million years old! The crystal dome at Mystic Caverns is eight stories high. Miles of trails wind through Blanchard Springs Caverns. It has some of the world's most spectacular rock formations.

▲ **Rock formations at Mystic Caverns**

▲ The Rosalie House in Eureka Springs is one of the town's many historic buildings that clings to the mountainsides.

Buildings in the hilly town of Eureka Springs cling to the mountainsides. Take the seven-story Basin Park Hotel, for example. Every floor is the ground floor! Each one exits onto the hillside.

Pea Ridge battlefield is the site of a fierce Civil War battle. Today, the park includes a section of the Cherokee Trail of Tears. This was the trail the Cherokee followed to Oklahoma when they were forced to move from their eastern homelands.

▲ **Pea Ridge Military Park in Rogers preserves an important part of Arkansas's history.**

Another furious Civil War battle raged at Prairie Grove, which is now a state park. The site's Ozarks village gives a glimpse of life in the mid-1800s.

How did pioneers make the things they needed? You'll see for yourself at the Ozark Folk Center in Mountain View.

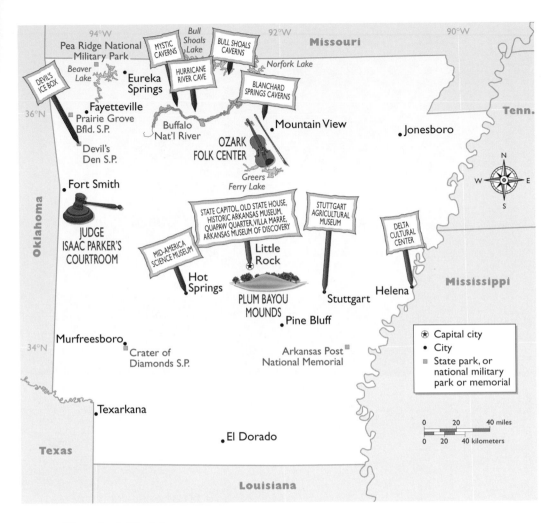

▲ **Places to visit in Arkansas**

Its craftspeople make soap, brooms, candles, and dolls.
They're happy to show you how they do it.

Suppose you were an outlaw in the late 1800s. You'd
know Fort Smith was not the place to be. You'd end up in
Judge Isaac Parker's courtroom. That meant you'd probably

be hanged. Called the "hanging judge," Parker sentenced eighty-six criminals to be executed. Today, you can see his jail, courtroom, and **gallows.**

In Little Rock, you can take a tour of the capitol and watch lawmakers at work. Nearby are the Old State House and the Historic Arkansas Museum. Little Rock preserves many historic homes in the Quapaw Quarter. One famous

▲ **One of many historic buildings in the Quapaw Quarter**

▲ **Yellow Bluff in Devil's Den State Park**

home is Villa Marre. It appeared on the television show, *Designing Women.* Stop by the Arkansas Museum of Discovery. Among other things, you'll discover what a lightning bolt feels like.

Would you like to build rivers and mountains, or make your hair stand out in all directions? Then you need to go to the Mid-America Science Center in Hot Springs. It's full of hands-on activities for exploring science. Do you enjoy hot baths? Take a soak in one of the city's hot-water pools. If you'd rather be cold, visit the Devil's Ice Box. It's in Devil's Den State Park. The "icebox" is a deep crack in the rock formations. It never gets above 60 degrees Fahrenheit (16 degrees Celsius).

Have you eaten any rice lately? It probably came from eastern Arkansas. There you'll pass acres of rice fields. The Stuttgart Agricultural Museum tells the story of the pioneer farmers. The Delta Cultural Center is in Helena. It explores Delta blues, frontier life, and Civil War days. Henri de Tonti founded Arkansas Post at a Quapaw village. Today, its museum traces the post's history from the 1600s.

▲ **Bull Shoals is one of Arkansas's scenic mountain lakes.**

Beaver, Norfolk, Greers Ferry, and Bull Shoals are some of Arkansas's clear mountain lakes. They're great spots for boating, fishing, and waterskiing. For a real boating adventure, try the Buffalo National River. Ancient cliffs tower over the gentle waters. Along the banks, the wilderness is alive with animals.

Floating along quietly, you'll notice the whispers of the woods and the gentle splash of the water. Then you'll know you're in a true Natural State.

Important Dates

10,000 B.C.	Paleo Indians arrive during the Pleistocene geological period.
700 A.D.	Mounds are built at Plum Bayou.
1541	Spanish explorer Hernando de Soto passes through Arkansas.
1673	French explorers Jacques Marquette and Louis Jolliet come down the Mississippi River and stop at the mouth of the Arkansas River.
1686	Henri de Tonti establishes Arkansas Post, Arkansas's first permanent European settlement.
1803	The Louisiana Purchase makes Arkansas a part of the United States.
1817	Fort Smith is established to keep peace among Native American groups.
1819	Arkansas Territory is created.
1836	Arkansas becomes the twenty-fifth U.S. state on June 15.
1861	Arkansas joins the Confederate States of America; the Civil War begins.
1864	A new constitution abolishes slavery.
1868	Arkansas is readmitted to the Union.
1921	Arkansas's first oil well is built near El Dorado.
1932	Hattie Caraway of Arkansas is the first woman elected to the U.S. Senate.
1957	The National Guard enforces a Supreme Court order for racial integration at Little Rock's Central High School.
1964	Orval Faubus becomes the first Arkansas governor elected for six terms in a row.
1978	William Jefferson ("Bill") Clinton is elected governor for the first time.
1993	Bill Clinton becomes the forty-second U.S. president.

Glossary

caverns—caves

delta—a fertile region near the mouth of a river

expedition—a long journey by a group of people to explore a region

gallows—a frame from which criminals are hanged

Hispanics—people of Mexican, South American, and other Spanish-speaking cultures

moonmilk—a white mineral deposit made of tiny crystals

mounds—hills made of earth or stones that are built over a burial or ceremonial site

plantations—large farms worked by laborers who lived there

wilderness—a wild, untamed area

Did You Know?

★ The name *Arkansas* is the French version of a Native American term. Illinois Indians called the Quapaws a name that sounded like *akansa*. It meant "people who live downstream."

★ Under Judge Isaac Parker, more people were executed by the U.S. government in Fort Smith in the late 1800s than at any other time in American history.

★ The average temperature of the springs in Hot Springs is 143°F (62°C).

★ Many famous people have enjoyed the waters of Hot Springs. They include President Franklin D. Roosevelt, gangster Al Capone, and baseball star Babe Ruth.

★ Stand in the middle of Texarkana's State Line Avenue. You'll have one foot in Arkansas and the other foot in Texas!

★ Pro-British forces called Tories attacked the Spanish at Arkansas Post in 1783 but were driven back. This was called the Colbert Incident and was Arkansas's only Revolutionary War action. It was also one of only two Revolutionary War battles fought west of the Mississippi River.

★ Blind folk singer Emma Dusenbury recorded 116 songs for the Library of Congress in the 1930s. She sang at the Arkansas Centennial in 1936.

State capital: Little Rock

State motto: *Regnat Populus* (Latin for "the people rule")

State nickname: The Natural State

Statehood: June 15, 1836; twenty-fifth state

Land area: 52,075 square miles (134,874 sq km); **rank:** twenty-seventh

Highest point: Magazine Mountain, 2,753 feet (839 m)

Lowest point: Ouachita River in Ashley and Union Counties, 55 feet (17 m) above sea level

Highest recorded temperature: 120°F (49°C) at Ozark on August 10, 1936

Lowest recorded temperature: -29°F (–34°C) at Pond, in Benton County, on February 13, 1905

Average January temperature: 40°F (4°C)

Average July temperature: 81°F (27°C)

Population in 2000: 2,673,400; **rank:** thirty-third

Largest cities in 2000: Little Rock (183,133), Fort Smith (80,268), North Little Rock (60,433), Fayetteville (58,047)

Factory products: Food products, paper products, electrical equipment, metal goods

Farm products: Chickens, rice, soybeans, cotton, catfish

Mining products: Natural gas, petroleum, bromine, crushed stone

State flag: Arkansas's state flag shows a diamond-shaped design in white with a blue border. It's displayed against a field of red. In the center is the word *Arkansas* with four blue stars. The diamond shape stands for Arkansas's diamond production. Within the blue border are twenty-five white stars. They stand for Arkansas's place as the twenty-fifth state.

State seal: The state seal shows an American eagle with a shield on its breast. In the shield are a steamboat, a beehive, a plow, and a bundle of wheat. They stand for Arkansas's industry and farm products. Above the eagle is the female figure of Liberty. On either side are the angel of mercy and a sword representing justice.

State abbreviations: Ark. (traditional), AR (postal)

State Symbols

State bird: Mockingbird

State flower: Apple blossom

State tree: Pine

State mammal: White-tailed deer

State fruit and vegetable: South Arkansas vine-ripe pink tomato

State insect: Honeybee

State rock: Bauxite

State gem: Diamond

State mineral: Quartz crystal

State musical instrument: Fiddle

State beverage: Milk

State American folk dance: Square dance

Making Chicken-Fried Steak

A favorite way to serve steak in Arkansas.

Makes four servings.

INGREDIENTS:

4 round steaks, about 1/2 pound each

1 cup flour

Salt and pepper

1 egg

2 1/2 cups milk, divided

1/4 cup vegetable oil

DIRECTIONS:

Make sure an adult helps you with the hot stove. Pound the steaks with a wooden meat tenderizer. Mix a little salt and pepper into the flour. Dip each steak in the flour mixture until they're covered on both sides. Lightly beat the egg. Mix it with 1 1/2 cups milk. Dip the steaks into it. Then coat them with flour again. Heat up the oil in an iron skillet. Fry the steaks until they're brown on both sides. Place on paper towels to drain. Now make the gravy. Remove all liquid from the skillet except for about 2 tablespoons. Stir in a little of the flour. Beat in 1 cup milk. Stir over medium heat until it thickens. Pour gravy over the steaks and serve.

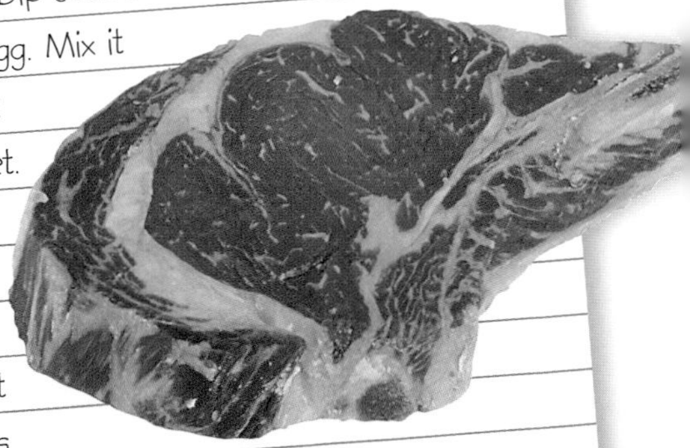

"Arkansas"

The state anthem is "Arkansas," with words and music by Eva Ware Barnett. Besides the state anthem, Arkansas has two official state songs. They are "Arkansas (You Run Deep in Me)," by Wayland Holyfield, and "Oh, Arkansas," by Terry Rose and Gary Klaff. Arkansas also has an official state historical song. It's "The Arkansas Traveler," a folk tune that became popular because of a story told by Colonel Sanford "Sandy" Faulkner.

I am thinking tonight of the Southland,
Of the home of my childhood days,
Where I roamed through the woods and
  the meadows
By the mill and the brook that plays;
Where the roses are in bloom
And the sweet magnolia too,
Where the jasmine is white
And the fields are violet blue,
There a welcome awaits all her children
Who have wandered afar from home.

Chorus:
Arkansas, Arkansas, 'tis a name dear,
'Tis the place I call "home, sweet home";
Arkansas, Arkansas, I salute thee,
From thy shelter no more I'll roam.

'Tis a land full of joy and of sunshine,
Rich in pearls and in diamonds rare,
Full of hope, faith, and love for the
  stranger,
Who may pass 'neath her portals fair;
There the rice fields are full,
And the cotton, corn and hay,
There the fruits of the field
Bloom in the winter months and May,
'Tis the land that I love, first of all, dear,
And to her let us all give cheer.

Famous Arkansans

Maya Angelou (1928–) is a poet and novelist. Her best-known work is *I Know Why the Caged Bird Sings.*

Daisy Bates (1914–1999) headed the NAACP during the fight to integrate Little Rock's schools. Her home is now a national monument.

Dee Brown (1908– 2002) wrote *Bury My Heart at Wounded Knee.* He was born in Louisiana and lived in Arkansas.

Helen Gurley Brown (1922–) was the editor-in-chief of *Cosmopolitan* magazine and is an author of many books. She was born in Green Forest and raised in Little Rock.

Eldridge Cleaver (1935–1998) was a civil-rights activist. He wrote the book *Soul on Ice.*

William Jefferson ("Bill") Clinton (1946–) was Arkansas's governor for twelve years. Clinton (pictured above left) was the forty-second U.S. president from 1993 to 2001.

John Gould Fletcher (1886–1950) was the first Arkansan to win the Pulitzer Prize. He won it for *Selected Poems* in 1939.

J. William Fulbright (1905–1995) was a U.S. senator from Arkansas (1945–1974). He was chairman of the Senate Foreign Relations Committee.

John Grisham (1955–) is a popular author. Many of his books have been made into movies, including *The Firm* and *The Client.* He was born in Jonesboro.

John Johnson (1918–) is a magazine publisher. He founded *Ebony, Jet,* and other black-oriented magazines. Johnson is a native of Arkansas City.

Scott Joplin (1868–1917) is called the Father of Ragtime. He wrote popular tunes such as "Maple Leaf Rag."

Douglas MacArthur (1880–1964) commanded Allied forces in the Southwest Pacific region during World War II.

Winthrop Rockefeller (1912–1973) was Arkansas's first Republican governor (1967–1971) since Reconstruction. He was born in New York City.

Mary Steenburgen (1953–) is an actress. Her movies include *What's Eating Gilbert Grape?* and *Life as a House.* She is from North Little Rock.

Edward Durell Stone (1902–1978) was an architect. Some of his buildings are the Museum of Modern Art in New York City and the Kennedy Center for the Performing Arts in Washington, D.C.

Sam Walton (1918–1992), a Newport native, founded the Wal-Mart chain of stores. He opened the first one in Bentonville.

Want to Know More?

At the Library

Altman, Linda Jacobs. *Arkansas.* Tarrytown, N.Y.: Benchmark Books, 2000.

Di Piazza, Domenica. *Arkansas.* Minneapolis: Lerner, 2001.

Lucas, Eileen, and Mark Anthony (illustrator). *Cracking the Wall: The Struggles of the Little Rock Nine.* Minneapolis: Carolrhoda Books, 1997.

Thompson, Kathleen. *Arkansas.* Austin, Tex.: Raintree/Steck-Vaughn, 1996.

Welsbacher, Anne. *Arkansas.* Edina, Minn.: Abdo & Daughters, 1998.

On the Web
Official Website for the State of Arkansas

http://www.state.ar.us/
To learn about Arkansas's history, government, economy, and land

Arkansas: Vacation in the Natural State

http://www.arkansas.com
To find out about Arkansas's events, activities, and sights

Through the Mail
Department of Parks and Tourism

One Capitol Mall
Little Rock, AR 72201
For information on travel and interesting sights in Arkansas

Department of Arkansas Heritage

1500 Tower Building
323 Center Street
Little Rock, AR 72201
For information on Arkansas's history

On the Road
Arkansas State Capitol

Capitol Mall
Little Rock, AR 72201
501/682-6244
To visit Arkansas's state capitol

Index

Angelou, Maya, 29
animal life, 4, 11
Arkansas Folk Festival, 30
Arkansas Museum of Discovery, 39
Arkansas Post, 14–15
Arkansas River, 10–11, 19
Arkansas River Valley, 7
Arkansas Territory, 4
Arkansas-Oklahoma Rodeo, 31

Basin Park Hotel, 34
bauxite, 18
Blanchard Springs Caverns, 33
blues music, 29–30
borders, 6
Brock, Lou, 32
Brown, Dee, 29
Bryant, Paul "Bear," 32
Buffalo National River, 40
Bull Shoals Caverns, 33

Campbell, Glen, 29
Cash, Johnny, 29
caves, 33
Central High School, 19
Cherokee tribe, 15, 34
Civil War, 17, 34, 35, 39
climate, 11–12
Clinton, William Jefferson, 22
Crowley's Ridge, 9

Dean, Jay Hanna "Dizzy," 32
Delta Cultural Center, 39
Delta region, 8, 9, 10, 12, 25, 30

Devil's Den State Park, 39
diamond mining, 24

El Dorado, 18
ethnic groups, 28–29
Eureka Springs, 34
executive branch of government, 20, 21

farming, 8, 10, 15, 18, 25, 26, 39
fish-farming, 26
folk arts, 30
forests, 6, 8, 27
Fort Smith, 7, 15, 16, 28, 31, 36–37
France, 14
Fulbright, J. William, 22–23

Great Depression, 18
Greene, Bette, 29

Hendricks, Barbara, 29
Historic Arkansas Museum, 37
Hot Springs, 6, 39
Hunt, H. L., 18
Hurricane River Cave, 33

integration, 18–19

judicial branch of government, 20, 22

King Biscuit Blues Festival, 30

lakes, 4, 6, 11, 40
legislative branch of government, 20–21

Little Rock, 7, 18, 19, 21, 28, 37, 39
local government, 22. *See also* state government.

manufacturing, 4, 19, 26–27
marine life, 26
Mid-America Science Center, 39
Mills, Wilbur, 23
mining, 15, 18, 24
Mississippi River, 6, 9
Moncrief, Sidney, 32
Mountain View, 30, 35
mountains, 4, 6, 30, 35
Mystic Caverns, 33

national government, 22–23
National Wild Turkey Calling Contest, 31
Native Americans, 13–14, 15, 34, 39
natural resources, 8, 15, 18, 24–25
Nuttall, Thomas, 4

oil, 8, 18
Old State House, 37
Ouachita Mountains, 6
Ozark Folk Center, 35
Ozark Mountains, 6, 35

Parker, Isaac, 36–37
Pea Ridge battlefield, 17, 34
Petit Jean Mountain, 4
Pippen, Scottie, 32
plant life, 4, 6
plantations, 15–16, 17
population, 28
Port, Charles, 29

Prairie Grove, 17, 35

Quapaw Quarter, 37

Red River, 11
rivers, 6, 9, 10, 11, 19, 40

Saint Francis River, 10
service industries, 27
slavery, 16, 17
Sloan Site, 13
Soto, Hernando de, 14
sports, 31–32
state capital, 7, 18, 19, 21, 28, 37, 39
state government, 20–22. *See also* local government.
state nickname, 4
statehood, 16
Stuttgart Agricultural Museum, 39

Toad Suck Daze festival, 30
Tonti, Henri de, 14, 39
Tontitown Grape Festival, 31
tourism, 19
Trail of Tears, 34
Turkey Trot Festival, 31

Van Buren, 16
Villa Marre, 39

Walton, Sam, 27
White River, 10
World Championship Duck-Calling Contest, 30
World War II, 18

About the Author

Ann Heinrichs grew up in Fort Smith, Arkansas, and lives in Chicago. She is the author of more than one hundred books for children and young adults on Asian, African, and U.S. history and culture. Ann has also written numerous newspaper, magazine, and encyclopedia articles. She is an award-winning martial artist, specializing in t'ai chi empty-hand and sword forms.

Ann has traveled widely throughout the United States, Africa, Asia, and the Middle East. In exploring each state for this series, she rediscovered the people, history, and resources that make this a great land, as well as the concerns we share with people around the world.